This book is dedicated to Mrs. Johnson.

Copyright © 2025 Jennifer Jones
All copyright laws and rights reserved.
Published in the U.S.A.
For more information, email info@ninjalifehacks.tv
Paperback ISBN: 978-1-63731-978-9
Hardcover ISBN: 978-1-63731-980-2
eBook ISBN: 978-1-63731-979-6

Find the Cupid on Strike lesson plans at ninjalifehacks.tv

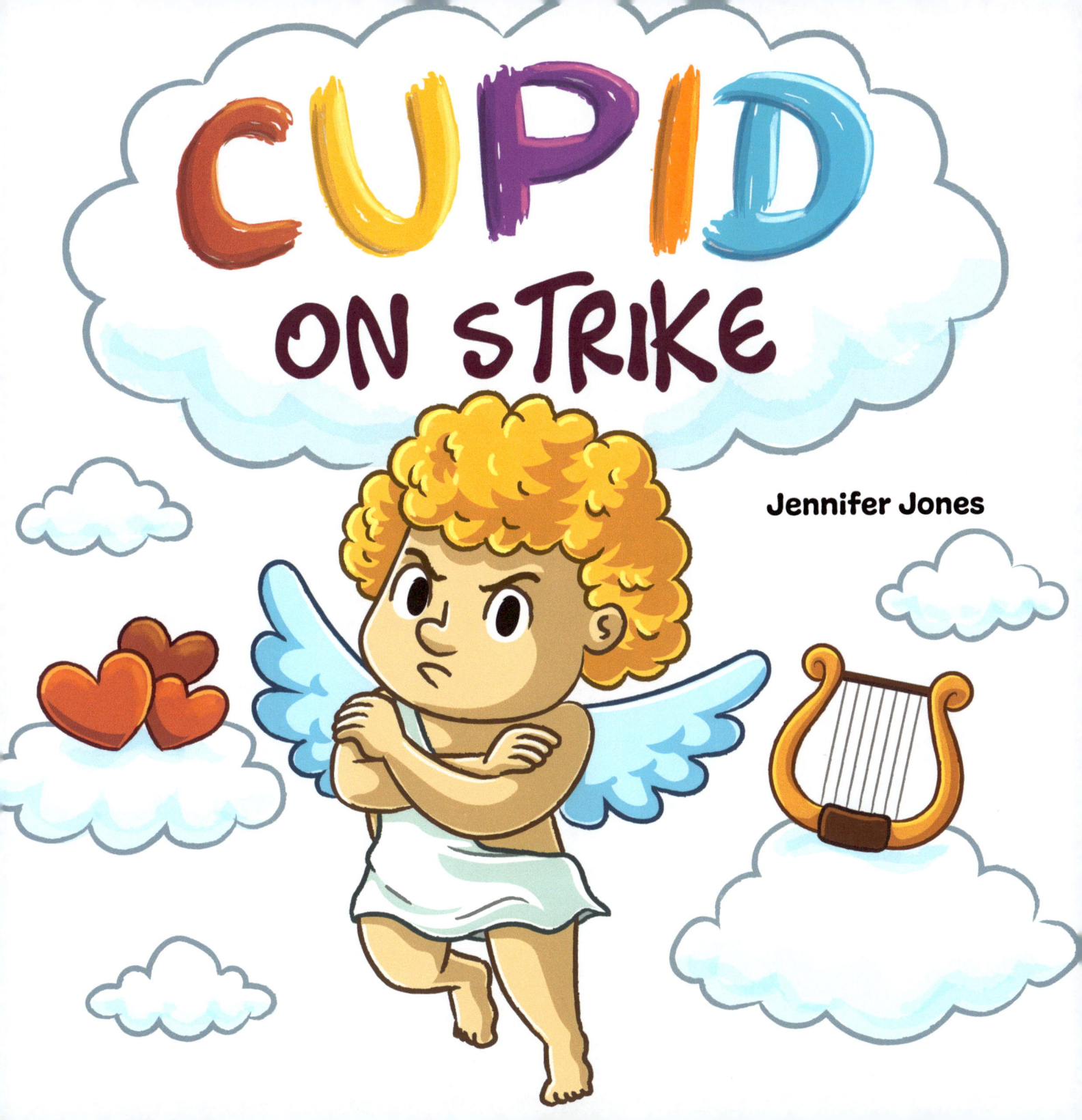

It started on a Valentine's Day
with laughter in the air,
with cards and sweets and silly pranks
and Cupid's worried stare.

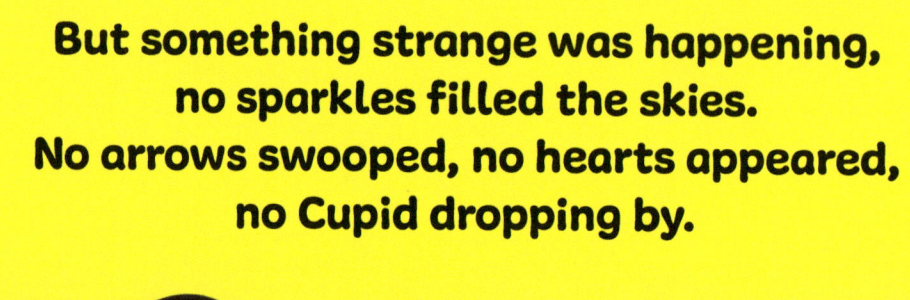

But something strange was happening,
no sparkles filled the skies.
No arrows swooped, no hearts appeared,
no Cupid dropping by.

Dear students,

Valentine's Day has slipped away.

It used to mean a day of love,

but now it's gone astray!

You laugh at cards that tease and prank,
you toss the notes we send.
You care more about lollipops
than kindness to a friend.

Miss Honey said, "Let's change it up and bring the love back in. Let's show Cupid we still care. We'll help the love begin!"

They made real notes with kind, true words
and gave out hugs and cheer.
They focused more on lifting hearts
than sweets and plastic gear.

Create a Real-Deal Valentine!

Write something kind for someone you care about.

Who it's for: _____
What makes them special: _____
_____
What I want to say: _____
_____
_____
_____

Draw a picture for them here!